*In celebration of the joys of being
the mother of Brennan, Kay Kay and Jake
and the daughter of Quentin and Bernice Ball.
- Crystal*

*For my children, Nathan Tillman and
Sara Frances who taught
me to appreciate the small
things all around us.
-Valerie*

This book is presented to:

_____

From:

_____

Date:

_____

Monarchs & Milkweed

Preserve and Protect

Jake and the Migration of the Monarch

Monarch Publishers, Permissions
400 North Main St. #405
Greenville, SC 29601

Copyright 2006
Second printing. Printed in Singapore by TWP

Library of Congress Control Number
PCN 2004110676

SUMMARY: Jake's mother teaches him that like the butterflies,
he can always find his way home.

ISBN 0-9774038-3-1
[1. Monarch butterfly. 2. migration, nature, family love, etc. Fiction.]

www.monarchpublishers.com

Crystal Ball O'Connor, Ph.D., Valerie Bunch Hollinger, and Monarch
Publishers have joined in dedicating a portion of the revenue from
Jake and the Migration of the Monarch to education projects that
support early childhood literacy.

Jake and the Migration of the Monarch

STORY BY CRYSTAL BALL O'CONNOR, PH.D.

PICTURES BY VALERIE BUNCH HOLLINGER

Monarch Publishers
Greenville, South Carolina

The sky wrapped its arms around the Carolina coast while Momma wrapped her arms around Jake. The blue rocking chair creaked on the porch where Mom and Jake rocked back and forth, back and forth.

A fluttering of color broke the silence.

"Look, Jake, a butterfly."

"Yes, Momma, and more!"

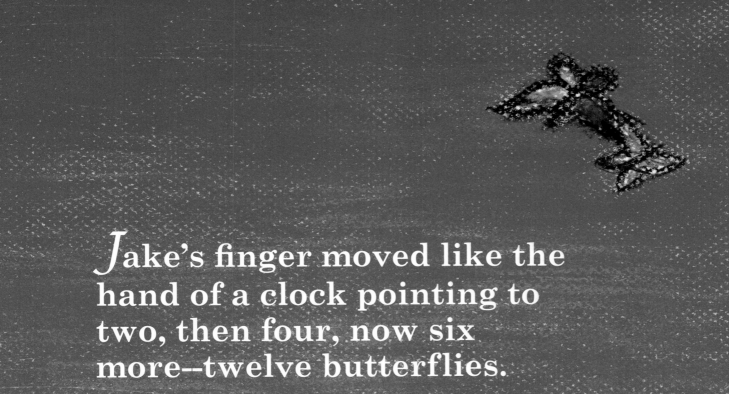

Jake's finger moved like the hand of a clock pointing to two, then four, now six more--twelve butterflies.

Momma's immediate thought as with dandelions, first stars, and birthday candles was, "Quick Jake, make a wish. Blow the fuzz off the dandelion!"

From the tall grasses and sand dunes the butterflies puffed up like dandelion seeds riding in the wind.

Jake always closed his eyes when he made a
wish. He pressed his open hands to the sky—
"I wish my hands could reach a butterfly cloud."

More and more
butterflies appeared.

Momma was joyful. This was a blessing. Snuggling Jake under her chin Momma said,

"You fill my heart like the butterflies fill the sky.

You give my heart wings.

For every butterfly I see, I'll make a wish in your name."

Butterflies flickered in the sky like daytime stars.

Like constellations, the butterflies took the shape of Orion the Hunter with three bright stars to make a belt.

More butterflies became The Big Dipper and The Great Bear. Splashes and circles spread far and near.

Jake wondered aloud in a little song:

*"Butterfly, Butterfly way up high
What's it like to kiss the sky?"*

At first the butterflies looked like small black specks. As they swarmed closer, Momma and Jake saw orange, and moving black stripes. "Monarch butterflies," Momma said quietly in Jake's ear.

Those that flew low came right by the porch, almost close enough to touch. "Jake, see the bright orange and black?" Momma whispered. "The colors of the monarch butterfly send a message to larger insects and birds.

If a bird takes a bite, the butterfly tastes really yucky and the bird says, 'No, thank you. No more monarchs for my lunch.'"

What a spectacular sight! Nature's grand parade of weightless wonders swirled around them. Momma called out as she and Jake watched the butterflies continuing toward them in great numbers. "Oh, Jake, we're in the middle of the migration of the monarch!"

"They fly from Canada and the northern part of the United States to spend their winter in a warm, cozy climate. This is called migration, Jake. Some monarchs fly thousands of miles to make this trip."

"Momma, can we please just watch butterflies today? I don't want to miss a single one." Momma paused for a moment. "Let's take it as it comes."

She put her "Things to Do" list in her pocket and replaced it with Jake's hand. "Yes, dear. We can stay and stay."

As hundreds more butterflies floated into view and disappeared, Jake sang again:

"Butterfly, Butterfly where will you go? And what shall you do when you get there?"

Momma snuggled Jake even closer. "Every fall they fly to a particular place in the mountains of Mexico. They do not really have a map, but they know how to get into the wind that will take them exactly where they want to go. In this special place in Mexico you can see millions of butterflies covering the trees and the ground. With the butterflies, the world is wearing its fanciest clothes."

"The trees and mountains are just right to protect the butterflies from wind and cold. Mist in the clouds and rolling fog help them get enough water to drink. The surroundings are perfect to keep the butterflies safe. That's why we help take care of the water and earth and air -- so the monarchs and all living things can have what they need to survive."

A thousand butterflies later, Jake ran into the
courtyard facing the water and pretended
to have wings.

He became a monarch butterfly,
dancing in circles for a while,
then darting in different directions.
First, here. Now, there.

The song continued:

"Butterfly, Butterfly what will you do
When wintertime is through?"

"They save up all their energy and strength until spring and then, the butterflies begin the long journey back to the United States.

They lay their eggs on only one kind of plant, the milkweed, before they die. This creates a new generation of monarchs."

"*J*ust imagine, this time next year their great grandchildren will fly along the Carolina coast heading south to spend winter in Mexico."
"Will they have a map?"

"No," said Momma. "But they will know how to find their way. The sun is their compass and the mountains their landmarks."

"Each generation is very important to the next in many ways," Momma explained.

"*J*ust as your parents and grandparents and great-grandparents help set a path for you, the butterflies do the same thing."

The bright warm fall day was now turning to cool evening. Momma told Jake that butterflies fly only during the day, so they knew it was almost over.

Jake sang the final verse of his song:

"Butterfly, Butterfly
   have a safe flight.
We'll watch you
   and watch you
'til day turns to night."

They did just that. They watched, straining their eyes until the last of the butterflies could be seen. They couldn't be sure which one would be the final butterfly, so each butterfly took on greater importance in the dimming of the day around Momma, Jake and their butterflies.

They were happy that they'd watched until the last butterfly disappeared into the soft darkness. Jake returned to Momma's lap and told her, "Butterflies will always make me think of you, Momma. Now it's your turn to make a wish."

Momma closed her eyes and then opened them again smiling:

"Like the beautiful monarch butterfly,

May you always know how to get into the wind that will take you where you want to go.

May you find a special place to keep you well.

And, My Dear Child,

May you always, always find your way home."

Monarchs and Me . . . .

*H*ow we are given our names can help tell the story about what makes us special.

The word monarch means "ruler" or "king." During the monarch's magical metamorphosis from egg to caterpillar to chrysalis to butterfly, the light green chrysalis is adorned with a line of golden beads making the shape of a king's crown.

*P*arents, grandparents and great-grandparents help in the journey. The new generation begins the cycle of life again, continuing the path of those who came before and those who will follow.

Several generations of summer monarchs live only two to six weeks. The migrating monarchs are different. They live about eight months and migrate south to find just the right conditions to survive the winter. Monarchs born west of the Rocky Mountains overwinter in California. Monarchs born east of the Rockies or in Southern Canada migrate to the Sierra Madre mountains of Mexico.

Though they have never been there before and they have no map, they fly thousands of miles to find the same oyamel fir tree forests visited by their great-grandparents the year before. In spring they begin their journey north to find a mate and lay their eggs before they die.

*E*ven a weed can be beautiful and essential.

Without milkweed, monarch butterflies cannot survive. Monarchs lay their eggs only on milkweed leaves, and baby caterpillars only eat milkweed. The milky white liquid in its leaves protects monarchs by making them poisonous to predators. Often milkweed is cut down or killed because it is a weed. Instead, we can plant more milkweed and help others understand its importance.

*B*utterflies and people need the care and help of others to survive.

Let the monarch butterflies' Spanish name, mariposas monarcas, remind us that the local people of the mountains of Mexico are trying to conserve the forests needed to protect monarchs even though they can use the firewood from the trees to earn money to feed their families.

Please visit *www.monarchpublishers.com* to learn more about the world of monarch butterflies. A host of educational and entertaining resources are offered free of charge. The site includes outstanding teacher guides to help meet national standards in a variety of subjects, including the performing arts, and fascinating activities for children and parents.

......Our Family Tree

My Name

_____

Father   Mother

_____   _____

Grandfather   Grandmother   Grandmother   Grandfather

_____   _____   _____

Great-Grandmother   Great-Grandmother

_____   _____

Great-Grandfather   Great-Grandfather

_____   _____

Great-Grandmother   Great-Grandmother

_____   _____

Great-Grandfather   Great-Grandfather

_____   _____

How I Got My Name

_____

Oyamel Fir Tree

Jake's Song

Words by Crystal Ball O'Connor, Ph.D.
Music by Sharon Kazee